HANDSHAKE *with* NATURE

KELECHI LUMENZE

PARTRIDGE

Print information available on the last page.

To order additional copies of this book, contact
Toll Free 800 101 2657 (Singapore)
Toll Free 1 800 81 7340 (Malaysia)
orders.singapore@partridgepublishing.com

www.partridgepublishing.com/singapore

CONTENTS

"GOING GREEN" AND THE NEED TO SUSTAIN OUR ENVIRONMENT

By Lumenze Kelechi

From the phrase itself, one could easily sense or imagine what it entails, as green is a color that represents life, it symbolizes nature, Agriculture, yield and productivity. Green revolution has to do with the mindset, it doesn't have to come as an elephant project, because it deals with our environment, the environment is us, and we are the environment, because we deal with it in our day to day lives.

For humans to strike a balance in a sustainable environment, there is urgent and natural need to be friendly to the ecosystem and biological diversity, so as not to overwhelm or suppress the strength of eco support in providing the needed and necessary services to meet human needs. Environmental sustainability has been talked about by different schools of thought, industries and even politicians. Yet human attitudes, behaviors and actions seems to be in contravention to the principles of nature.

1

According to Brundtland Report 1987, titled **Our Common Future**, prepared for the World Commission on Environment and Development "sustainable development is development that meets the need of the present without compromising the ability of future generations to meet their own needs". From the definition of this report, one can vividly understand that sustainability is a continuous process, something that, after someone will continue to exist, something that will continue to exist after a particular government, whatever policy or program any particular government initiated without putting into consideration the future wellbeing of her citizens and generation to come, is not sustainable in any sense. In my native Igbo culture, we have a surname system that every male born bears his father's surname, and this runs in the linage of every family, from generation to generation. This is referred to, in my native language as '**AHAMEFUNA**', which means upholding something so it doesn't get lost, forgotten or go into oblivion. This serves as a constant reminder, of whom one is, where one is coming from and heading to, and what one's family represents and is known for. It gives one the consciousness of who he or she really is, and that makes one to carry the symbol of the family with pride, and to ensure it continues to generations after him. That is why in Igbo culture, generations of a particular family still bears a single surname as an identity.

This I honestly think, is what the idea of Environmental Sustainability should be or look like, the word 'Environment' is encompassing, unfortunately some people erroneously think it has to do with just forests and biodiversity. And that is why most Government policies and programs are failing, because those in positions of authority, be it the Executive,

Legislature or Judiciary, fail to understand that the policies of Government, Acts of parliament and Judicial pronouncement or precedence have direct impact in determining how sustainable the Environment can be, Economically, Socially, Politically and otherwise.

In as much as we do what we do to meet our immediate and daily needs, for food shelter, clothing, leisure and other activities that adds value to our lives, we should be conscious not to cause damage to our environment or drain what we can not replace or renew.

EFFECTS OF ENVIRONMENTAL SUSTAINABILITY

ECONOMIC EFFECTS

Apart from the Ecology, Environmental sustainability has enormous impact on a nation's economy and contributes a lot to the economic prosperity of the local people, which is manifested in various forms... it could be counterpart funding of a project, public-private partnership, governmental funding to cottage industries, bailouts, cooperatives, bank assistance to businesses, bank to individuals, business to business, all these environmental sustainable development goals and many more has effect on the economic effect of the local people. When there is prosperity in the economy, it shifts the attention of people and government from Environmental damage and depletion to preservation and conservation. It creates more jobs and business opportunities. Government must ensure adequate security for businesses to flourish, improve infrastructure, guarantee the safety and protection of human right, especially foreigners. these attracts foreign direct investments, and leads to expansion of businesses.

Empowerment programs by Governments and NGOs aimed at improving the economic wellbeing of the people should be encouraged. Environment sustainability leads to job creation which translates into creation of wealth, it greases the wheel of economic development and makes the people to be eco friendly. By been eco friendly, people tends to preserve and conserve their natural resources, which boost soil fertility and crop yield.

At some point in the history of my country, cash crops was the major foreign exchange earner, due to utilization and quality management of ecosystem. Unlike today, that the government concentrates its focus on oil resources, which is causing great harm to the environment as a result of excessive explorations. Today we have environmental degradation, continuous lost of aquatic life due to oil spillage, soil infertility, water pollution, air pollution. In most cases, you discover that the amount of damages we cause to our environment far exceeds the gains and profits we derive from it.

These are the dangers of investing government fund in projects that will further sink the economy of a nation, a governor in the Eastern Nigeria, built 27(General Hospitals) in the 27 local governments that made up his state, without equipments, yet they were commissioned as completed. Now tell me, of what purpose are these hospitals to the masses? Even if they were 100% equipped, who are going to patronize these hospitals, is it the old men and women in the villages, who are predominantly farmers? When there are patent medicine stores and primary health centers in the villages. to have at least three well equipped general hospitals in each of the three senatorial zones is more reasonable than having 27 unequipped hospitals. All the fund invested there, automatically becomes a waste of resources, that would have been used to impact on the economic wellbeing of the people.

Our leaders should learn to have the interest of the people they are leading at heart, I believe that is why there is provision for them to appoint advisers in the cabinet, who will bring to bear their intellectual acuity and technocratic acumen in running the affairs of the government. Such sensitive appointments shouldn't be made on political considerations, but cut across political, ethnic and religious divides, considering how sensitive they are to the economy of a particular state or nation.

SOCIAL EFFECTS

When we talk about the social effects of environmental sustainability, we are referring directing to the people's wellbeing, needs and desires. The interaction between the people and the environment and how it affects them. In other words, you can not talk about the wellbeing of the people without mentioning the economic and environmental aspects of sustainability due to their interconnectivity. Whatever harm done to the environment backfires on the economic wellbeing and social security of the people.

Governments should come up with rules and laws that will regulate human activities and interactions with the environment, for instance logging of trees by the multinationals, it should be done selectively so as to maintain the forest diversity in order to preserve the fertility of the soil. When the environment is mismanaged, and the forest abused, the people will suffer the consequences. When the soil fertility is affected, crops will not have good yield, this may result to scarcity and inflation. When erosion sets in, there will be no road access for the people to do their businesses. If there is no more tree in the forest to regulate the water circle, automatically there will be climate change, which might be harsh to both the people and their farm produce.

In the energy sector, Government should develop a workable bill that will regulate properly the operations of mining activities, so it doesn't harm the environment. Oil spills poses a grave danger to the aquatic lives, it destroys farmlands by affecting the soil fertility, most times it leads to inferno in the forest when heavily heated by the sun. Oil pipelines should be well laid, across nonresident areas, the local people should be equipped with necessary skills on the local refining and production of the resources, as well as on the environmental safety and maintenance of the operations. These and other environmental friendly laws will not only guarantee the safety of the people but their social wellbeing.

Autonomy should be exercised by, or granted to the Local Governments, because it is the most closest tier of government to the people in relation to the environment. To deal with social issues at the top is entirely different if it is dealt with at the bottom which is the local government. While the former is acting in response to situation, the latter will not only work towards controlling the outbreak of a situation, but will create a kind of safety net and shock absorber incase of outbreak to avoid escalation.

Under primary health system which is usually under the administration of Local governments, the primary aim of the health care system is prevention rather than treatments of ailments. I remember when I was a child, the health care center staffs are always mobile, moving from door to door, house to house to administer vaccines and immunize the kids from contagious disease, so you can see that there administration is more of pro-activeness compared to the central government reactive measures.

The Local governments deals directly with the communities, and are in a better position to inculcate proper orientation to the people in relation to how to interact with the environment to make it sustainable.

Photo credit: pexels.com

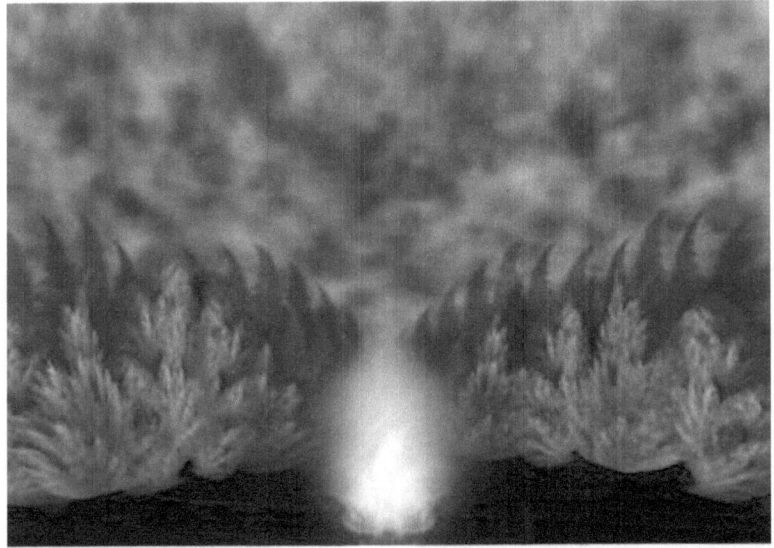

Photo credit: freepik.com

Industries and companies should have as their core values, Cooperate Social Responsibility (CSR), which enables them to give back to their host community and contribute to the sustainability of their host environment. By creating jobs for the people, drilling of bore-holes, holding seminars for environment sustainability awareness, liaising with the Government in it's drive to ensure a better living and environment for the people.

ENVIRONMENTAL EFFECTS

The environment has enormous effects on the people, because there will be no environment without the people. Let's take for instance, raising up kids where nature is nurtured, you will discover that the kids will grow up with the mindset of care and tolerance, and this also will affect their social life. My nephew in Indonesia, on his first day to school, flowers were giving to everyone of them. They were ask to go home with the flowers and return it after a giving period of time. The condition of the flowers upon return shall determine the mark that will be awarded to them. My brother, his father confirmed to me that, his son is becoming too attached to the flower that he would always check on it each time he wake up in the morning, whenever he return from school and before he goes to bed. And has already learnt to water the flower. In a sustainable environment, there is orderliness and sanity. When the environment is treated badly, a lot of social vices will arise, people will be forced out of their source of livelihood, due to scarcity, when this happens, they will resort to violence, some will pick up arms, then so many cases will follow suit, like kidnapping, terrorism, pipeline vandalization, food scarcity, hunger which in most case leads to protests and revolutions of the people against their governments.

In a sustainable environment, where there is good governance and effective legislation in place, enabling laws are put in place to regulate environmental operations by both the government, multinationals and individuals respectively. This goes along way in guaranteeing the economic prosperity of the people and stabilizing the economy of a nation. The operations of the industries that leads to the emission of unhealthy gasses in the air is regulated. There will be conducive condition of atmosphere, Agricultural and Natural resource will be well harness, ecotourism industry improved, there will be enormous job creation for the people, standard of living will improve, when all these and many more are in place, the lives of the people are positively impacted.

In a sustainable environment, Government policies and programs do have provisions for posterity, and not put the future of the younger generation in jeopardy. There is great need for the government to make Environmental sustainability, top priority in its agenda and development goals, as it has direct impact on the local people. Drilling and exploration of natural resources, especially mineral deposits, should be properly regulated, to avoid oil spillage and excessive industrial chemical waste. If these are unchecked, is capable of exterminating the aquatic lives of the environment and poisoning local people source of drinking water, damage of soil fertility which renders farm crops impotent and unproductive. And of cause you can imagine, the resultant effect, life expectancy of the local people will be affected.

GOING GREEN

Why do we really have to go green? people everywhere are talking about going green and it's effect on the environment. I mean people every day are trying to initiate better and ideal ways they can live a natural life. While there are many ways to do so, there are equally many reasons which are always forgotten. Understanding the reasons and importance of this current universal phenomenon will hopefully leave one with no option but to follow the trend.

Going green is never imposed on anyone, but a personal choice that is welcomed by everyone to support and maintain a good planet and make the world a better place to live for future generations. There are many good reasons why "going green" has become a symbol of environmentalism so clearly that it has generated a lot of curiosity among the people, I equally wondered how it developed and became so strong in the English language.

According to **Senator Ernest Gruening**, a Democrat from Alaska, "Every once in a lifetime in the history of mankind, a book has appeared which has substantially altered the course of history," so does "Silent Spring" by Rachel Carson in the

1970's. This is a philosophy which is predicated on a solid foundation of environmental sustainability.

Some understand this as keeping the environment clean, it goes far beyond that. It deals with the preservation of our natural resource, so as to create a sustainable environment. When we talk about the environment, we don't just mean our forestry, but entire bio-diversity, which connects everything that has to do with nature, the equatic life, animals and plants alike e.t.c.

BIODIVERSITY

Photo credit: freepik.com

Biodiversity is the absence of uniformity in every sense of it, it means different types and kinds of life on earth, with no form of consistency. That is why we have different species of plants and animals, with different weather conditions under which the various species survives most.

My late father once told me, "although one can not lay claim on the originality of this earth, but seeing the beauty of nature and how orderly the creations are, one will have no option but to accept the believe that there is a God, who indeed is behind all these".

IMPORTANCE OF PRESERVING BIODIVERTY

PLANT:

Deforestation:

Photo credit: freepik.com

As you may probably know, "Deforestation" is the destruction of trees so as to make land available for other uses. Modern day deforestation is a major problem due to destruction of trees, the rate is so vast, that over 2000(two thousand) trees are been cut down permanently every day.

According to National Geographic Wild, "scientists predicted that trees will go extinct within the next one hundred years".

This could cause a terrible effect on humans, because the trees that have been cut will no longer produce the much needed oxygen.

Deforestation alters people's traditional way of living, especially those that depends on rainforest for medicine, food, and shelter. It causes erosion which is the washing away of soils, by flowing rapidly with the rain water, when this happens it weakens the soil structure, which most probably leads to erosion.

Photo credict: freepik.com

Thousands, if not millions of our animal species goes into extinction or rather will go into extinction because there will be no place for them to live anymore. Animals that depends on plants for survival will die in the process for lack of food due to cutting down of trees. According to Michigan school of Natural Resources and Environment "habitat loss due to deforestation is the leading cause of extinctions. With the invasion of human development into their natural habitats, species have a harder time meeting their basic needs, such as shelter, places to raise their offspring, and sources of food and water. A reduced ability to survive and even mass extinction are often the consequences."

It causes lack of water in the atmosphere. Trees by nature controls the amount of water in the atmosphere by helping to normalize or regulate the water circle. With little or no tree in existence, as a result of deforestation, the air will have less water to return to the soil, which leads to dryer soil and crop impotency.

RUGA which stands for rural grazing settlement for migrant farmers, if not properly managed could lead to a major deforestation. Using my country Nigeria as a case study. As far as I know, Ruga settlement policy initiated by the federal government at the time was a good step, but in a wrong direction. It was a misplaced priority.

At a time when the world is seeking alternative energy to petroleum resources, when scholars are yearning for a paradigm shift from over reliance on mineral resources to cash-crops as it were in the early 70's when Agriculture was major foreign exchange earner.

Nigerians said NO to Ruga, because already the nomadic herdsmen have started grazing their cattle on people's farmland without their consent, leading to destruction of lands and crops, and of cause you do not expect people to fold their arms and watch their investments and source of livelihood go down the drain without speaking up or resisting such reprimand on their ancestral farmland.

Although there is nothing wrong proposing for settlement for pastoral farmers, but every thing is wrong grazing these cattle on people's domestic and commercial farmlands.

However, with good policies and programs, these issue can be easily addressed. These cattle can be resettled in the Sahara desert in Africa, is all about commitment and government taking it up as a priority. After all it has been proven scientifically that a desert can become fertile if adequately watered. Ranches can be built there, and herders could also lists their cattle online for people to order, pay and have their order shipped and delivered to them.

Unfortunately, the government of the day is not treating the issue with a kid glove, which made the conflict between herders and indigenous people to keep escalating by the day, leading to bloodshed and massacre of innocent people, in the Western, Eastern and South-southern part of the country. Today it has taking a different dimension because the herders are acting on a very wrong impression, that the have the backing of the Federal Government, which is what it seems. When a certain group of people are using dangerous weapons and fire arms to intimidate other group of people, to encroach and forcefully take over people's ancestral farmland, and yet government pretends nothing is happening, it portray such government as been partial and one sided in handling the affairs of a nation.

Today it has become a do or die affair, because the indigenous people are resisting such with everything they have, in other ways, they cant simply give up what rightfully belongs to them. I am taking my time to highlight on this point, because it is what is going on in my country, at the time of writing this book, this is what happens when Ruga settlement as a policy is wrongly formulated, and applied. And I wish that the Government, not just of my country, but other countries of the world could learn from this and avoid future danger that it portends, and its' reoccurrence, as in the case of Nigeria.

Right now, it has shifted from environmental to human disaster, which is a very bad omen. It has reached to it's crescendo, you can imagine a situation where the nomadic herdsmen now carry fire arms, such as AK47 and other sophisticated weapons to kill innocent people whose land they trespassed, not only killing them but also set their homes ablaze, attack their places of worship, young people loosing their lives in numbers, the girls been raped, pregnant women slated and their unborn babies, as if it is a state of war.

Now I am not trying to indulge into politics or take side, the emphasis am trying to make is that adequate government policies and programs can ensure a peaceful sustainable environment and control all these outbreak of conflicts, especially where there is diversity,

The solution lies in the government to employ rules and laws that will govern deforestation activities. Deforested trees should be replaced by planting younger trees. Commercial logging of trees, especially by the multi-nationals should be done selectively so as to maintain the diversity of the forest.

Pastoral farmers, especially nomadic herdsmen should be resettled far away from indigenous farmlands. So as to avoid destruction of people's farm crops and land damage.

Tropical rainforest is the most complex and diverse ecosystem, and sustains the largest concentration of biological diversity, that is half of all the plants and animals on earth. Whether you are someone who is on a tropical vacation, or someone who is environmentally conscious, it is up to us to act now and preserve our trees by recycling, using our forests sustainably and creating a protected environment.

THERE ARE SO MANY WAYS IN WHICH WE CAN "GO GREEN"

Reducing the use of tissues/papers...this reminds me an information posted at my college, tagged, **'Go Digital'** by my college head of studies/academics, **Ms. Indubalah Krishnan**. in fact, I must confess it was this bit of information about **paperless society** that actually formed my choice of this topic **'going green'**, during one of the public speaking competitions conducted by my college, in which I took first position. At our institution of learning, the use of papers, especially for printing of study hand-out, exam questions, writing of reports, projects and thesis by the students, posting of circulars can be replaced digitally. Students should be encouraged to toe that path, considering the fact that, the world is now a global village. Every bit of information is now on the internet which is now easily accessible. School managements should develop software for all their academic related concerns. You may be wondering, what has tissues/papers got to do with going green...a lot, in fact, everything because the primary source of these two products came directly from the forest timbers, and it is only by reducing their usage that we can be able to preserve the forest timbers and conserve our natural resources. For example, Bamboo tree

Photo credit: freestockphotos.biz

According to research, bamboo leaves have enormous health benefits.

Photo credit: freestockphotos.biz

Bamboo tree is multi-functional, especially the leaves. It's medicinal usage can not be over emphasized. Most of it's essential contents can not be found in other plants. It is very common in Asian countries, especially China. Bamboo tea is made from tit's leaves, we shall also take a look into some of its health and medicinal benefits

Removal of placenta: this is an organ inside the womb through which a developing baby is fed. When the bamboo tree is boiled and taking while hot by woman after putting to bed, the placenta is flushed out. It is also helpful to women to overcome menstruation challenges, as well as reduces pains during childbirth.

It is used to treat worms in the intestine, as bamboo leaf contains germs deadly to body parasites such as threadworms.

Studies shows that bamboo leave has a cooling effect in our body, which quenches internal heat in the stomach and heart. It is also used to boost fertility in men, as well as to cure erectile dysfunction.

Bamboo leaves is used to reduce and regulate the level of sugar in our body system. It contains low calorie, which helps to prevent overweight.

Bamboo plants regulates the level of cholesterol in the body system. Tea made from bamboo leaf help to cleanse the stream of our blood. It is used for treatment of different types of deceases due to it's content bamboo biomass

Protecting our natural habitats, such as animals.

although it is been argued by some people that "Deforestation" is an agent of development as it paves way for industrialization and commercialization, but I strongly believe that deforestation does more harm than good to our environment.

Photo credit: freepik.com

Deforestation causes loss of the natural home of animals, it is a complete destruction to our biodiversity, which is the largest concentration of half or more than plants and animals on earth. High specie density of animals are found in the tropical rainforest. One can not deny the fact that plants and animals can not be separated from the forest ecosystem, which provides enormous ecosystem related services to humans.

Humans will find it very difficult to survive without the existence of forests. Cutting down of trees in the forest not only lead to animal and specie extinction, but also cause climate change. Majority of our wildlife depends on the trees for food and shelter. And this is as a result of misplaced priority, especially by developing countries. There shouldn't be any need for unhealthy competition in the global economy between the poor and rich countries. I believe that each country should be unique for something.

If country A is known for technological advancement, country B is famous for scientific exploration, country C, if adequately endowed with natural resources, should strive to preserve and conserve it so that it could be known for something. I remembered in the 80's when a developing country was said to had used crude oil to exchange for services rendered to her by a technologically advanced country. This is what is referred to, in economics as the principle of comparative cost advantage. Although I perceived it as an act burn out of ignorance on the part of the developing nation, if only the leadership realizes the real value of crude, as it could be used to refine more than ten different petroleum products. However, to an extent it served a purpose. The point am trying to make is that there should be proper plan to contain the effects of deforestation, so that it will not be devastating to our biodiversity and forests as well.

Without the presence of trees to regulate the water in the atmosphere, the heat of the sun will be trapped on earth, and that will lead to climate change, automatically deforestation is one of the major causes of greenhouse effect and global warming.

Let us look into the effects of deforestation on Animals:

The consequences of deforestation on animals are enormous. When trees in the forests are cut, the natural habitat of the wildlife is not only degraded but also lost. By the removal of trees and other vegetations, their sources of food and shelter are reduced, which forces them to scatter and go extinct, and most of them die in the process. Desertification of their habitat makes them to become vulnerable to harsh weather conditions, and predation among others. Animals whose survival depends on any particular tree or forest growth will find it difficult to survive in other forest habitat.

Deforestation is a major cause of climate change, when trees are burnt for example, the carbon dioxide in their storage are released into the atmosphere, when this happens the earth becomes defenseless to the presence of heat from the sun, and this affects the climate by increasing the temperature, which makes life unbearable to most of the wildlife.

Deforestation is like a vicious circle, where one can not eat his cake and also have it. The trees that we destroy, there are animals that depends on them for survival, and there are also other ones that depends on the animals which depend on the trees for survival. When we cut these trees, the herbivores are endangered, and when the herbivores couldn't survive it or die as a result of starvation, the same fate will equally befall the carnivores which depends on herbivores for survival.

Endemic animals which are the most affected species of animals, automatically goes into extinction or die due to their inability to cope or survive in other habitats. For example,

Red Kangaroo

Photo credit: pexels.com

Red Kangaroo, scientifically called "macropus rufus" is a specie of animal endemic to native of marsupial Australia.

This is the largest of all kangaroos and has a unique feature, it leaps six feet high. Although they do avoid much fertile lands, as well as rainforest, the same thing is also applicable to animals endemic to rainforests, such as Jaguar:

Photo credit: freestockphotos.biz

Proper emphasis should be made on the need to preserve and conserve our forests, especially by the government. This will go a long way in inculcating on the mind of younger generation to be environmental friendly. Seminars, conferences, symposiums should be organized from time to time, the ministries, departments and parastatals of Agriculture and Natural resource should as a matter of urgency come up with environmental friendly policies and programs. in the institutions of learning, kids should also be thought on how to be friendly with nature, it is a thing of the mind, and once such orientation is giving a priority, people will also grow with the same mindset.

I remember a government program once initiated by the government of my country, tagged, "one child, one tree", and palm trees were distributed to all schools. I remember as a child I brought mine home, my parents had to take it down to the country-side, our home town to plant and it is still been harvested up till today. Now that was a good step in the right direction, because whenever we travelled to our home town, the first thing I would desire was to see how the palm tree was faring, even as a child I would take out weeds around it's root and water it. With such sense of care and nurture, I wouldn't want it to fade away. Growing with this kind of mindset, if I should find myself in any position of authority, especially in the government, of cause I will ensure that importance is attached in handling the affairs of our natural environment and it's habitats.

Ecotourism activities should be developed and harnessed by the government to give a boost to forest and biodiversity conservation. It should equally be encouraged in all levels of education, economic opportunities should be provided for people that depends their livelihoods on forest activities, this will help to conserve the forests, instead of exploiting it.

Humans also have their own share of the consequences of deforestation.

Photo credit: freepik.com

According to United Nations' Food and Agriculture Organization, "over 7 million hectares of forest are lost every year to human activities. The problem of deforestation is worsened by the rise of industrialization".

Deforestation alters people's way of living, as it is one of the causes of internal displacement and destroys people's source of livelihood. Research has it that over two billion people depend on the forests for food, shelter, medicine, drinking water as well as clothing e.t.c.

A lot of people predominantly live in the forest, deforestation causes erosion, which is the washing away of the soil nutrients.

The moment trees are cut, the roots loose its grip on the soil, thereby rendering it week and vulnerable to rain water, landslide will occur, which causes the soil to flow together with the rainwater. Apart from the soil losing its nutrients, people's places of abode, such as houses, farm lands, crop bans and other economic means of livelihood are totally destroyed. Erosion is a bane to development, it makes roads or places inaccessible due to landslide, the indigenous people affected will be totally cut off and isolated. Harvested crops will be wasted as there will be no means of marketing them.

It reduces the fertility of the soil, thereby making farm crops not to be productive.

Photo credit: freepik.com

Photo credit: freepik.com

Encouraging chain reaction, giving support to our local businesses. These businesses are likely to support other businesses within the environment, conduct their businesses in an environmentally responsible way, and most of all, generate employment within the local economy.

Maintenance of body fitness through Walking or biking. By biking, I mean bicycle and not power bike or motorbike...it sounds funny, but it is a fact of life. It saves energy and cost, it improves the condition of our heart and blood vessel by making them function properly, as well as reduces the risk of fat or overweight in our body system.

The last but not least, by eating home and organic food/ supporting our local farmers. This leads to conservation of biodiversity and goes in line with organic farming standards, today, due to over-reliance on foreign-made, the reverse is the case as the food we eat today are in most cases not healthy for consumption, due to distance the food travels before getting to us and unnecessary excessive preservation. By patronizing our local farmers, we will boost our agricultural sector, add momentum to the green movement and keep money circulating in our local economy.

WHY ARE GOING GREEN AND SUSTAINABLE ENVIRONMENT SO IMPORTANT?

Their importance can not be over-emphasized: Going green reduces utility bills, which in turn conserves our energy resources. It reduces global warming and green house effects, when trees are preserve, it properly regulates water cycle and adsorbs the heat from the sun. by using hand dryers in public places and offices, such as wash rooms and eatery, it will reduce the use of tissues and papers which automatically leads to the preservation and conservation of our forest trees.

Commercial logging of trees will help to maintain and balance the diversity of the forest. Soil fertility will be intact, and this will make farm crops to be productive. The biodiversity will not be threatened, and that will make the environment habitable for various species of both plants and animals.

Going green ensures lesser pressure on the exploration of the natural resources, especially mineral deposits, this reduces the level of oil spillage to the barest minimum. It's revives the aquatic life, and also protect the environment from degradation.

By harnessing the natural resources, local businesses are resuscitated, which keep money flowing in the economy. Sustaining the environment guarantees a brighter future for the younger generation, through government environmentally friendly policies and programs. Jobs will be created, human capital well harnessed.

we can not preserve our standard of living as human beings, the multiplicity of life in our planet, or Earth's biological community unless we welcome it. There are signs from all angles pointing to the fact that this natural phenomenon, going green and environmental sustainability are something that mankind must address. Otherwise, We will be in shortage of natural fuels, such as crude oil, natural gas, and coal e.t.c. Lots of animal species will go into extinction. We will lose our timbers in particular and forestry at large. We will destroy the atmosphere to the extreme... If we don't change.

And the only way to effect that change is by comprehending and struggling for sustainability—in our places of abode, in our social unit, in our biological community, and around the world.

SUMMARY

Going green is the key to a sustainable environment! Reduce, reuse and recycle are the big reasons why the earth goes green. Going green will help us and keep the earth safe.

There should be greater emphasis on the biodiversity, not just on its preservation and conservation, but on its sustainable usage through International collaboration and assistance.

Government should make adequate provision for the local farmers, both financially technically and otherwise. As well as come up with a viable and practical Agricultural and environmental policies and programs, so as to enhance Agricultural development.

Degraded ecosystem should be rehabilitated in a productive way, so as to make it attracting and competitive in nature, that way people including foreign investors will have confidence to invest and boost it's production.

Government should establish environmental research centers, so as to respond to environmental challenges and subsequently prevent any activity that will lead to it's degradation.

Priority should be given to human development, that way, poverty level of the people will be reduced to barest minimum. Natural resources suffers abuse in the hands of people, due to excessive poverty, there is hunger, and that is why the biodiversity is in jeopardy.

let us strive to save our environment from further degradation before it's gone. **LUMENZE KELECHI**